DECENTLY & IN ORDER

DECENTLY & IN ORDER

Bob Yandian

WHITAKER HOUSE

Unless otherwise indicated, all Scripture quotations are from the King James Version (KJV) of the Bible. Scripture quotations marked (NIV) are from the Holy Bible, New International Version, © 1973, 1978, 1984 by the International Bible Society. Used by permission.

Editor's note: This book has been edited for the modern reader. Words, expressions, and sentence structure have been updated for clarity and readability. Even at the cost of violating grammatical rules, we have chosen not to capitalize the name satan and related names.

DECENTLY AND IN ORDER

To contact the author:
Bob Yandian Ministries
P.O. Box 55236
Tulsa, OK 74155
phone: 1.800.284.0595 • fax: 1.918.250.0058
e-mail: bym@grace-fellowship.org • web site: www.precepts.com

ISBN: 0-88368-732-8
Printed in the United States of America
© 1983, 1987 by Bob Yandian

Whitaker House
30 Hunt Valley Circle
New Kensington, PA 15068
web site: www.whitakerhouse.com

Library of Congress Cataloging-in-Publication Data pending

Contents

Chapter 1

The Source of Authority in the Local Church

Chapter 1

The Source of Authority in the Local Church

Whenever you study, you should start with the source. It is the same way when we study church government. We should go to the source. When some people want to start a church, they run around to see how this church is set up, or how that church is set up. But we should go to the Word of God to find out how God wants His church to be established.

People who have awakened to the authority of God's Word today realize that God's Word works for healing just like it works for salvation. However, there is one thing you have to realize when you read the Word of God on any particular subject: God gives us guidelines and principles in His Word, but He leaves the responsibility of how to apply those guidelines and principles to us.

Let us look at the area of healing. The Word of God tells us that Jesus took our infirmities and bore our sicknesses, but it does not tell us exactly how to receive that healing. I have heard of people who learned that you have to "stand" on the Word to be healed. They believed exactly what they heard, threw their Bibles on the ground, stood on them, and got healed. But that does not mean that you will get healed if you go home and put your Bible on the floor and stand on it.

I have heard of other people who have shouted at their disease or sickness and have been healed. On the other hand, I have heard of people who have prayed silently to the Lord and have received their healing. The principle for receiving healing is to release your faith and to believe the truth of God's Word. The principle is not to do what somebody else has done. Not everyone has to dip in the Jordan seven times to be healed. In the ministry of Jesus, we see that not every case was handled the same. If they had been, we all might have to get mud or spit rubbed in our eyes to get healed.

What is it, then, that we want to look for in God's Word? Is it the example or the principle? It is the principle.

Let me give you an illustration that shows the danger of following someone else's example. I heard of an evangelist in Texas to whom God spoke very specifically out of the Scriptures. He read how Jesus spat on the ground to make mud for the man's eye, and the Lord told him to spit on people and they would be healed. Well, if you run around spitting on people, you better be sure you have heard from God.

We need to learn that the Holy Spirit speaks to us individually about His Word. We have to seek the principles by which the Word works. That is what we are going to be looking at concerning the subject of local church government. What are the principles God has set forth for the purpose of establishing and running His church? First, let us start with the most basic question: What is the church?

The Church

There are many Scriptures that refer to the church. I want to begin with 1 Corinthians 12:27–28.

Now ye are the body of Christ, and members in particular. And God hath set some in the church.

We are going to see this Scripture several times for different reasons, but let us limit our interest right now to the word *"church."* Today we use the word *church* loosely. Most people think of a building when they hear the word. But a building is nothing more than brick and mortar. In fact, you could walk out of the building after holding a church service, turn it into a disco, and you would not change the building. We often say, "I'm going over to the church." The accurate way to say it would be, "I'm going over to the building that houses the church."

Then what is the church? We are. The universal church is made up of every born-again believer on the face of the earth. Every group of believers who worships together is a segment of the universal church. Those segments that meet together are local churches.

But, you might ask, what does the word *church* really mean? In 1 Corinthians 12:28, *"church"* comes from the Greek word *ekklesia. Ekklesia* comes from another Greek word *ekkaleo. Ekkaleo* is a compound word. It is made from two words: *ek-* and *kaleo. Ek* means "out," and *kaleo* means "to call." Thus, what the word *church* really means is "the called out ones." Another way to say it is "the chosen ones," and it was translated that way in Ephesians 1:4. When Paul said we were chosen in Him before the foundation of the world, the same word is used *(ekkaleo)*.

What we want to keep in our hearts is that we study the Word of God to learn of Him and to be made more like Him. I believe that God has shown me some important things about Himself, about the Lord Jesus Christ, and about our relationships with Him and each other. If you will really open your ears and listen to what the Holy Spirit wants to say, it will change your life. It all starts and ends with this one word, *church*: the called out ones, the chosen ones.

The Caller and the Called

I want you to get a point deep down inside you, so follow my reasoning carefully. The church is called out, right? "The called out ones" means two things. First, there is someone doing the calling. Second, there is someone receiving the call. Notice that to receive the call is to respond and not just to hear. If the church is the "called out" or "chosen" ones, there has to be someone calling or choosing.

First Corinthians 12:28 says, *"God hath set some in the church."* Who is doing the calling? God is.

Let us look at another Scripture that deals with the same subject. Ephesians 4:11 says, *"And he gave some."* To understand who *"he"* is, we have to go back a few verses. If we start in verse eight, we see a passage Paul quoted from Psalm 68:18:

> *Wherefore he saith, When he ascended up on high, he led captivity captive, and gave gifts unto men.*

Who ascended up on high? Who gave gifts to men? The Lord Jesus Christ. Let us see what it goes on to say in verses nine and ten:

> *(Now that he ascended, what is it but that he also descended first into the lower parts of the earth? He that descended is the same also that ascended up far above all heavens, that he might fill all things.)*

Notice that verses nine and ten are in parentheses; this means that verse eight takes up again in verse eleven. Jesus ascended, and then He gave gifts to men. Verse eleven tells us what the gifts are: apostles, prophets, evangelists, pastors, and teachers. Here in Ephesians 4:11 the Lord Jesus Christ is the One who sets ministry gifts in the church. In 1 Corinthians 12:28, God the Father is the One who sets the ministry gifts in the church.

Ministry gifts are chosen by God the Father and the Lord Jesus Christ in combined authority. They work together in authority, not independently.

Galatians 1:1 makes this point very clear:

Paul, an apostle, (not of men, neither by man, but by Jesus Christ, and God the Father, who raised him from the dead.)

Paul declared that he was an apostle, and he makes us understand who is responsible for making apostles. Notice that he said that *"men"* (plural) were not responsible for his becoming an apostle, neither was it by *"man"* (singular). So, no group of men and no individual man can choose and create an apostle. Only the Lord Jesus Christ and God the Father can choose and create a minister.

Again, let us read what those ministry gifts are in Ephesians 4:11.

And he gave some, apostles; and some, prophets; and some, evangelists; and some, pastors and teachers.

Jesus is the One who calls and appoints the ministry gifts, and I want to emphatically point out that there is no mention of the words *bishop, elder,* or *deacon* in this list of ministry gifts. The Word of God does talk about bishops, elders, and deacons, but they are never listed with the ministry gifts, which are called by God the Father and the Lord Jesus Christ.

The most important point I want you to see from these Scriptures is this: The One who does the calling has authority over the one He calls. Whoever chooses the ministry gift has authority over the one who is chosen. Who is the head of the church? Look at Ephesians 1:22–23.

> *And hath put all things under his feet, and gave him to be head over all things to the church, which is his body, the fulness of him that filleth all in all.*

Jesus, the Lord Jesus Christ, is the Head of the church. He was given that position by God the Father. He has authority over all the ministry gifts He chooses. He was given the authority over the church by God the Father.

Well, if the Lord Jesus Christ does not choose bishops, elders, or deacons—they are not listed with the ministry gifts chosen by Him—who does? This is the gray area of church government today and the subject of this book. We will discuss the pastor's office first, then the church offices of elders, bishops, and deacons.

The Pastor–Shepherd

The Greek word for *pastor* is *poimen*. It is the same word translated *shepherd*. *Shepherd* and *pastor* are the same word in Greek. So what is the implication? Do shepherds have more than one flock that they watch at the same time? No. A shepherd or a pastor can watch only one flock at a time. A pastor is the only ministry gift given to the local congregation. He is called and chosen by God the Father and the Lord Jesus Christ for a local congregation. He, the pastor, is responsible to the Lord Jesus Christ directly, because the One who calls has authority over the ones He calls.

What about the other ministry gifts? Where do they function? From scriptural examples we see that apostles can come from a local church like Antioch (Acts 13:1–3; 1 Corinthians 12:28), but they travel, establish churches, and minister to the entire body of Christ. Prophets can also come from a local church (Acts 11:27; 13:1), but they are for the entire body, not just the local church. They go many places in their ministry. The evangelist also travels many places preaching the gospel. Evangelists and pastors traditionally have been well-known ministries, but today the teacher is widely known in the body of Christ. The teacher is also for the body as a whole. Thank God for the teachers we have today. However, let me reemphasize that none of these four gifts is for a local group of people in particular.

In my own case, I moved from the ministry gift of a teacher to the office of a pastor. I do not consider that a step down; I consider that a step up. Every time you move in the ministry, you never go down; you are always promoted for your faithfulness. When you prove yourself in one office, God promotes you to another.

I began as a Sunday school teacher, but I did not stand in the office of the teacher. That is important: Not all teachers stand in the office of a teacher. When God moves you into a ministry office, He accompanies it with spiritual gifts. Supernatural signs accompany each ministry office.

I taught in the Sunday school on Sunday evenings for five or six years, and a good-sized group began to develop. The more I taught, the more I began to see in God's Word. I moved closer and closer to the time when God put me in the office of teacher. It was not something I asked for; God just gave it to me. I knew down inside me that I was called to the office of a teacher, though no one ever said it to me. There are some things it is good to keep to yourself and let God prove to others.

When I was ordained into the ministry in 1977, God confirmed the call through someone else. At that time, I had hands laid on me, and a prophecy was given stating that I was called to the teaching ministry. The Lord said I had cried in the night because of the revelations He had given me in His Word, but I had no place to give them. That is exactly what I had done, but I did not tell anyone. So you see, man does not make a ministry gift, God does. He may confirm it through prophetical gifts. You know inside that it is true, but it is reassuring to have the confirmation. Now, I am a pastor, and God is confirming it with the supernatural abilities of the Holy Spirit.

Let me make another point about the pastor and the congregation. God calls a pastor to the congregation He wants him to shepherd. Just as sheep are put under a shepherd by their owner, so God chooses the pastors for his flocks. When a congregation votes on a pastor, they must realize that they are not choosing their pastor; they are signifying that the Holy Spirit bears witness to them that this is God's choice. They do not select; they acknowledge and accept God's selection.

Gifts to the Local Church

The ministry gifts listed in Ephesians 4:11 are called the five-fold ministry gifts, and they are repeated in a slightly different form in 1 Corinthians 12:28. I want to point out again that bishops, elders, and deacons are not listed with those ministry gifts. The source for ministry gifts, according to the Word of God, is the Lord Jesus Christ. Where, then, do bishops, elders, and deacons originate in the church?

Let us examine several Scriptures to find the answer. First, let us consider Acts 14:23:

> *And when they* [Paul and Barnabas] *had ordained them elders in every church, and had prayed with fasting, they commended them to the Lord, on whom they believed.*

Paul and Barnabas were the ones who ordained the elders. In what office did they both stand? They stood in the office of apostle. In chapter one of

Galatians, Paul declared that. Who chose Paul? There can be no controversy about Paul's direct call by the Lord Jesus Christ. Who had authority over Paul? Jesus, who called him, had authority over him. The principle should be clear. Those in ministry offices choose the elders; therefore, they have authority over them. It is a simple delegation of authority. Let us see another example.

Titus was a young minister. He had come up under the ministry of Paul. He was Paul's trouble-shooter. If Paul had any trouble in a church, he was able to send Titus in and know that things would get straightened out. Paul had sent Timothy to Corinth to try to bring order into the church, but he failed. Then Titus was sent. In chapter eight of 2 Corinthians, we see that Titus then took the problems and began to work them out. The church straightened out. You remember that the Jews did not like Titus because he was an uncircumcised Gentile, a Greek (Galatians 2:1–4). But the ministry gift of God was in him, and the signs and wonders worked through him. This was God's seal of approval. Religious people have a hard time coming against the supernatural.

At another time, Paul left him in Crete to pastor. He said this in Titus 1:5:

> *For this cause left I thee in Crete, that thou shouldest set in order the things that are wanting, and ordain elders in every city, as I had appointed thee.*

I am not going to define the office of the elder at this point. I want to show who chooses him and his relationship to that one. Where do elders come from, and to whom are they responsible? Who has authority over them? Just as the pastor is chosen and called by Jesus and is under His direct authority, the elders are under the authority of the ones who choose them. Elders in this case were chosen by someone in a ministry office and were under his authority. It is a clear scriptural pattern. The pattern is a simple chain of command.

We see that elders are appointed by men in ministry offices and are under their authority. What is the source for the office of bishop? We will define the office and function of the bishop later, but now let us look to the Scripture to find where they originate. Look at Philippians 1:1.

> *Paul and Timotheus, the servants of Jesus Christ, to all the saints in Christ Jesus which are at Philippi, with the bishops and deacons.*

There is only one pastor (shepherd) for a congregation (flock), but there is a plurality of bishops. Furthermore they are separated from the offices of Paul and Timothy and mentioned with the congregation (saints) at Philippi and also the deacons.

> *This is a true saying, If a man desire the office of a bishop, he desireth a good work.*
> (1 Timothy 3:1)

This office does not come as a divine call from God. It is something to which a man aspires. It is something he desires to be. It is said to be a good work, but it is not something that can be equated with the call of God to the full-time ministry.

What about deacons? Where does their office originate? Who chooses them? Who exercises authority over them? Look at Acts 6:5–6:

> And the saying pleased the whole multitude: and they chose Stephen, a man full of faith and of the Holy Ghost, and Philip, and Prochorus, and Nicanor, and Timon, and Parmenas, and Nicolas, a proselyte of Antioch: Whom they set before the apostles: and when they had prayed, they laid their hands on them.

"And they chose." Here, "they" refers to the whole multitude or congregation of believers in Jerusalem. It is clear from these verses that the congregation chooses the deacons in the local church. Then the ministers confirm their choice through the laying on of hands. Who then has authority over the deacons? The congregation does. Notice that it does not say that the deacons were chosen by the apostles or the pastor. If that were true, the deacons would serve the pastor. The deacons are set in the congregation to serve the people. They are servants of the people. Another point to notice is that the way the deacons were chosen is not specified; therefore, each congregation may choose as they think best.

The important aspect of deacon selection, which is equally true for the selection of elders, is that they meet the qualifications established by the Holy Spirit in God's Word.

Chapter 2

Traditional Forms of
Church Government

Chapter 2

Traditional Forms of Church Government

I n the discussion that follows, my intention is not to judge one form of church government as superior or inferior to another from a natural point of view. Rather, I want to find and point out what form is in agreement with the Word of God, the Bible. There is one reason for that: If you want a supernatural church, you must have biblical authority for your church government. Signs and wonders will become commonplace when your house is in order.

There are four main types of church government in the body of Christ today: episcopalian, presbyterian, congregational, and independent. The title tells us who is in authority.

Episcopalian Church Government

The episcopalian form of church government is found in many types of churches: the Roman Catholic, the Anglican, the Episcopalian, the Methodist, the Lutheran, and the Churches of God. The title points out who has authority: the bishops.

The Greek word *episkopos* (translated episcopalian) means "an overseer" or "a bishop." When you see the word *bishop* in Scripture, it means the overseer. Another word to use might be *superintendent*.

In the episcopalian form of church government, the bishop *(episkopos)* has the authority, and the pastor is under him. Now according to what we have studied, does this form of church government conform to the biblical standard? If it does, then you can say it is a correct form of church government for the body of Christ. If it does not, then you have to say it is unscriptural; it is wrong.

The first denomination that I pointed to was the Roman Catholic Church. The Roman Catholic Church employs the episcopalian form. Its line of authority begins with the highest-ranking bishop, the pope. Under him is the cardinal (cardinal bishop). Under the cardinal bishop is the archbishop. Under the archbishop is the bishop. Under the bishop is the local bishop. Under the local bishop is the priest or pastor. The pastor (priest), who, by biblical authority, is directly under the Lord Jesus Christ, is under the authority of five bishops above him, who are chosen by men.

Also remember that God's Word tells us that the office of a bishop is something to which a man aspires. Accordingly, we have five offices chosen by man above the office chosen by God. Does that make sense? Not biblical sense. It comes from a misunderstanding of the term *bishop*. Bishops are in the Word of God and are ordained by God. But they do not rank with the ministry office of the pastor. The Word of God does not say that Jesus Christ gave apostles, prophets, evangelists, pastors, teachers, and bishops. We must let God's Word be the guide and judge of correct church government.

Presbyterian Church Government

The Greek word from which we derive the word *presbyterian* is *presbuteros;* this is where we get the word *elder.* When we find the word *elder* in the Bible, it comes from the Greek *presbuteros.* One place the word is used is 1 Timothy 4:14:

> *Neglect not the gift that is in thee, which was given thee by prophecy, with the laying on of the hands of the presbytery* [the elders].

In this form of church government, the authority for the local church rests in a group of elders. This type of government is found in the Presbyterian Church, the Pentecostal Holiness, the Friends, and many non-denominational churches. The church is governed by a group of elders. Traditionally they number seven, ten, or twelve.

In this form of government, the elders are over the pastor, or the elders and the pastor have equal authority. But in God's Word, who chooses pastors? The Lord Jesus. Who should choose elders? The pastor. Does it sound right that the ones the pastor chooses should exert authority over him? Should the ones chosen by men rule the one chosen by God?

The Word shows that God chooses a pastor as head of the local church. Whenever there is a multiplicity of people in authority in a church, they usually have to vote to find God's will. Elders are necessary for counsel to the pastor, but not to make his decisions for (or with) him. *"In the multitude of counsellors* [not voters] *there is safety"* (Proverbs 11:14). (See "What about Church Boards.")

Congregational Church Government

By this title, we can see that the congregation has the authority. Voting is the means by which most all decisions are made. The major denominations that have congregational church government include the Baptists, the Assemblies of God, the Churches of Christ, and the Congregationalists.

An interesting fact about congregational forms of church government is that they arose about the time the United States became a nation, two hundred years ago. Apparently it was presumed that if we have a nation run by the will of the people, then we should have churches run by the will of the people. The authority rests with the congregation. Is this a proper form of church government? No, not according to the Word of God.

People will argue with you by saying that this is a form of government that works in the United States. Democracy does not make the church possible; the church makes democracy possible. The church is not a natural institution, but supernatural. It must be run supernaturally from the standards of God's Word, not history books.

If we want to cite precedent, we ought to look at God's Word and see how He established the nation of Israel. He established one head over all. Then He divided the nation into smaller groups (tribes) with overseers under the authority of the head (Moses, or a king). For example, Moses, as the head, led the nation of Israel directly under God's authority. Then there were men responsible for tens, hundreds, and thousands under him. But they still came under Moses and submitted to his authority (Exodus 18).

The reason some of these forms of church government came into being was out of an abuse of authority by the pastor. The presbyterian form of church government arose because a pastor was not fulfilling his office properly. A group of men (elders) arose and exercised authority over him to protect the congregation. When the elders began to abuse authority, the congregation as a whole decided to take the authority away from them. But even the congregational type of government is also subject to being swayed by one man's opinions or influence. No matter how we look at these attempts by men to prevent abuses, they still occur. God's Word is still our guide. His choice is to have one man who hears Him rule over the church.

He is not a dictator, but a shepherd who leads his flock with sound counsel.

Independent Church Government

The independent form of church government is the closest to the precedent set in God's Word. In this form of church government, the church is governed much like a corporate business. The pastor is like a president and the elders are like vice-presidents. Nevertheless, there is only one head to the organization, the pastor (president) of the church.

Now, does the Word of God teach a multiplicity of elders? Yes, it does. Notice what James 5:14 says:

> *Is any sick among you? let him call for the elders of the church.*

Notice that *"elders"* is plural, and *"church"* is singular. In the local church, there can be a number of elders (Acts 14:23). But who chooses the elders? The pastor does (Titus 1:5). Who has authority over them? The pastor does. We are not talking about authority in a natural sense of understanding. We are talking about divine authority, which comes from the throne of God to the people through a ministry gift chosen and equipped by the Lord Jesus Christ. This must always be kept in mind whenever there is a discussion of scriptural church authority. Remember that God says in Romans 8:7 that the carnal mind is an enemy to God. If we want God present in our lives, then we have to live in line with His Word. And if we want God present in our churches, then we have to get our churches in line with His Word.

What about Church Boards?

I strongly believe in the authority of the pastor, but not unlimited authority. There must be a system of checks and balances in a church just like a business, marriage, or other institutions.

Husbands are the final authority in the marriage, but not to the extent of committing adultery with no recourse for the wife. *"Moses because of the hardness of your hearts suffered you to put away your wives* [divorce]" (Matthew 19:8).

Because pastors also can become hardhearted and leave the lifestyle and doctrinal principles of the Word, protection must be built in for the people. "Church Board" is not a bad phrase.

Because boards have dominated churches, choked the creativity out of pastors, and stopped the move of the Spirit does not mean we throw out the baby with the bathwater.

A pastor with unlimited authority and a church dominated by a board are both playgrounds for satan. There must be a balance.

First, there must be a process for acquiring a pastor, either a board of mature men, a congregational vote, or both. Should the pastor abuse his

office, the same process that put him in should
remove him.

Let us create a good example. A group (board)
of men find a pastoral candidate who seems to bear
witness with them. They bring him in for a few
weeks to speak to the people, and they sense God's
call on this man to be their pastor. A church-wide
vote is taken on a set Sunday, and he is elected by
an eighty-percent majority. (There are always those
who would not recognize God if He sat next to
them).

Once in office, the pastor should be free to run
the church as he sees fit. The vote delegated authority
to him.

When there was no pastor, the board was the
authority. Now that a pastor is in his scriptural office,
the board should switch to a limited position. As
long as the pastor's life and teaching remain in line
with God's Word, the board's primary function is
to advise. The board becomes a buffer between the
pastor and congregation. Its members can advise him
as to people's attitudes and feelings on particular
subjects. They also can give him business information that he or his staff do not know. The board is
advisory only. The pastor still makes the final decision.

One area the advisory board should have power
over is the pastor's salary. A pastor should not desig-
nate his own salary. He should set pay scales of all

staff below him but not his own. He should feel free to voice his opinion on his salary but leave the final decision to the board.

The advisory board should be considered elders. They do not stand in the office of an elder (those who rule and teach—see "Qualifications for Office—Elder and Bishop"), but they should be mature in the Word, in love, in care for the congregation, and in respect for the pastor's office.

They are chosen by the pastor (Acts 14:23, Titus 1:5). Therefore, when a new pastor comes to office he may want to change them after he has become familiar with the church operations. He may also want to change any or all of the staff, those who stand in the office of elder. He is the authority and this is his prerogative.

If the pastor abuses his authority established by the standards of God's Word, the advisory board should take authority to protect the congregation. The abuses should be apparent and blatant. They should fall under two categories: morals and/or doctrine. If the pastor were to be unfaithful to his wife, steal money from the church funds, be caught in a crime, or any other serious violation, the board should step in.

If he were to blatantly teach doctrines contrary to the faith, the board should take authority here also. To teach against the Virgin Birth, divine healing, or salvation by faith would be some of the areas. Small areas of disagreement will always arise but should never constitute grounds for dismissal.

The advisory board should also give ample opportunity for repentance on the pastor's part. They should treat him as the Lord treats us (Matthew 18).

If the pastor is caught in flagrant opposition to the Word and does not desire to repent, the matter should be taken to the people for a vote. The ones who voted him in should vote him out. This is all the voting that should ever be done.

The process would begin again. The advisory board (perhaps with the staff's help) would find a candidate (possibly an associate on staff) for the congregation to vote on. Once God's man is found and put into office, the board goes back to an advisory role only.

So many boards these days want to maintain a hold over the new pastor. They fear he may make some mistakes, and they want to protect the church. The basis for any healthy relationship is trust, not fear. Give him the full reins. Do not make him pay for the mistakes of the previous pastor. He may become discouraged and eventually leave, thus justifying the board's fears and causing even more pressure on the next pastor.

Boards that have control or equal authority with the pastor will always slow down the progress of the church. Most boards I have seen in churches are made up of businessmen in the congregation. They meet once or twice a month to make decisions concerning the business and direction of the church. They do not live with the church problems each day and are therefore uninformed. The first thirty minutes to an hour are used for catching up on a month's happenings from the pastor, who feels frustrated about having to report to this group. They then spend hours discussing trivial details that the staff pastor could have remedied in ten minutes.

The reason decisions take so long is because few on the board want to accept responsibility for a wrong decision. No one will make a firm decision. The buck is passed instead of stopped. Decisions are shelved until the next meeting and the pastor goes back to his office with little accomplished. Items such as carpet colors, drapery fabrics, and choir robes are caught in a maze of confusion. The reason no one will accept responsibility is that they fear offending the congregation. Their public acceptance is more important than progress.

Many boards are dominated by one or two strong-willed people. We are back to one-man rule when this happens. Why not make him the pastor?

Neither the universal church nor the home is run by a board. The local church is compared to both. How would you husbands like your home run by a group of men outside your family? They can meet only once a month, and you have either an equal voice or none at all. All problems must be held until the monthly meeting and must be presented to a group that does not live with your problems as you do from day to day.

The home is the training ground for handling the local church, the family of God.

For if a man know not how to rule his own house,
how shall he take care of the church of God?
                                        (1 Timothy 3:5)

Chapter 3

Analogies for Church Government

Chapter 3

❦

Analogies for Church Government

Whenever God is establishing principles in His Word, He always does so in more than one way. We have seen how Scriptures give instructions about lines of authority; now I want you to look at two verses that give us analogies for the church.

Whatever applies in the universal church can also apply to the local church. Why? Because the pastor holds the same position in the local church that the Lord Jesus Christ does in the universal church.

Remember that the Lord is called the Chief Shepherd (the same word as pastor). Because the Lord Jesus is chief pastor, the local pastor is under His authority. The local church is a visible pattern for us to understand the universal church. Let us examine Ephesians 5:22–23:

Wives, submit yourselves unto your own husbands,
as unto the Lord. For the husband is the head of
the wife, even as Christ is head of the church: and
he is the saviour of the body.

The key words in these verses are emphasized, and you might underline them in your Bible: *husband-wife, Christ-church,* and *head-body.*

The church spoken of here is obviously the universal church—all believers around the world. The important point is that they all come under the headship of the Lord Jesus Christ. He is the Head of the church.

"Head" represents authority. Jesus is the One who has called us out. He is the One who has authority over us. The first analogy is of Christ as head over the universal church. That relationship of authority can be transferred to the local church.

The second analogy in these verses is of a marriage—the husband and wife. Not only are two separate people joined together as one, but the husband is clearly established by the Word of God as the "head" of the marriage. He has the duty of exercising authority in that union.

Notice in all three of these analogies, the word *head* is used. There is only one head to a marriage in God's plan.

What does this mean if the husband and wife are in contention over a point? Who should submit? The woman should submit whether she thinks she is right or wrong. If the husband makes a mistake, let him make it. Sometimes that is the only way for him to learn.

The third analogy for the local church in these verses is the human body. The head is the control center for the human body. The body does not function without the head.

An obvious point should be brought up here. Although the body is under the rule of the head, this does not mean that the head never listens to the body. The five senses are in the body to counsel the head. They send signals to the head at all times. I can reach out with my finger and get information. The message races up to my head, and my head makes the decision to move the finger or not. If the head makes no decision, the hand gets burned. But my head will also suffer when my hand is hurt. The head never disregards any part of the body or is careless about its welfare.

The same principle is true in the local church. We can see in all three of these analogies that God has one source of authority. The marriage has one head. The body has one head. The universal church has one head.

God's plan is for the local church to have one head, the pastor. Many think that when a church becomes large, it needs more than one pastor. That is like saying that if a family has many children, it needs another husband or father. If your body gets fat, it needs another head. If the universal church gets many more converts, we need another Jesus. No! If a family becomes large, the father delegates authority to the older children to watch over the younger. This is the role of the pastor and the elders in the local church.

In the family, the husband may make wrong decisions, but he is still the head of the family. You personally have made wrong judgments, but your head was not removed.

You may not always agree with the pastor's decisions, but he is still God's head of the local church. The pastor has a responsibility to the Lord Jesus Christ for the people.

The Pastor's Accountability

The pastor is responsible to the Lord Jesus for the people God has given him. Revelation 2:1–4 will show us that.

> *Unto the angel of the church of Ephesus write;*
> *These things saith he that holdeth the seven stars*
> [seven churches of Asia] *in his right hand,*
> *who walketh in the midst of the seven golden*
> *candlesticks* [ministers of the churches]; *I know*
> *thy works, and thy labour, and thy patience, and*
> *how thou canst not bear them which are evil: and*
> *thou hast tried them which say they are apostles,*
> *and are not, and hast found them liars: and hast*
> *borne, and hast patience, and for my name's sake*

*hast laboured, and has not fainted. Nevertheless I
have somewhat against thee, because thou hast left
thy first love.*

To whom is this indictment written?

If you say the church of Ephesus, you are wrong.
If you read the address at the top of this letter, it is to
the angel of the church.

What does that mean? Is this a heavenly angel?
Could He be talking to an angel in verse four when
He says that the angel has left his first love?

The Lord Jesus Christ is the One doing the talking. We can be assured that holy angels do not lose
their first love. God does not have anything against
His angels. The Greek word is *angelos,* and here
it has been translated, *"angel."* The word actually
means "messenger" and is translated that way in
James 2:25. Many other translations translate the
word as "messenger" here in this passage in Revelation, as well.

In light of all we have studied, who is the messenger of the church at Ephesus? The pastor is. He is
God's messenger to the people who make up the local
church.

God holds the pastor responsible for the error
that gets into his church. The pastor is the chief overseer for his church. He is responsible.

The people and the pastor become a reflection of
each other. Just like a married couple, they begin to

act and think alike after a number of years. The faults found in the congregation are put on the account of the pastor and God holds him responsible.

Notice that the angel or messenger is singular. John was telling us that over each church there was one pastor.

Each church was a different size but all were put under the headship of one pastor who was overseen by Jesus Christ, the One who walks among the candlesticks. Jesus inspects the churches and puts the blame squarely where it belongs—on the pastor, the head of each church.

Chapter 4

Authority with Love

Chapter 4

❖

Authority with Love

Peter told the pastors of his day, *"Feed the flock of God which is among you, taking the oversight thereof,...Neither as being lords* [dictators] *over God's heritage"* (1 Peter 5:2–3). Authority is something that must be exercised with boldness yet with love and concern for those in the congregation. A pastor is no more a dictator over the local church than a husband is over a family or Jesus is over the universal church.

There is a flow of submission and authority within the Godhead. The Holy Spirit is in submission to the Lord Jesus Christ, and the Lord Jesus is in submission to God the Father. Yet all three submit to each other when it is necessary. Out of this love relationship comes power. There can be submission and authority at the same time. This only occurs as equality is recognized.

Within the home, the father is the head of the family. If the wife or children do not agree with the father's decision, they still submit to his authority in love. If he exercises his authority in love, he will have the respect of the wife and children. If he is a tyrant, he will be able to command only obedience, not submission or respect.

Obedience without submission is slavery. In the end, he will defeat his own purpose and destroy his own position.

If the husband is making every effort to fulfill his role as head of the home, the wife needs to let him make mistakes when he gets bullheaded. Do not try to usurp his authority. Counsel and love him, but let him learn the hard way a time or two. He will come to value the wisdom and sensitivity of his wife in time.

Authority only exists and works when someone submits. Submission is the reception of authority.

Rebellion is the rejection of authority. Rebellion always leads to frustration and the breakdown of authority. Why is God opposed to rebellion? It is the sin of satan himself. It is defined in the Word as the sin of witchcraft.

Rebellion causes one of two things to happen. The person in the position of authority either loses his authority or tries to exert his authority with force. When the latter happens, the person in submission will either crack and come under authority against his will or rebel even more.

Do you see that rebellion at the bottom causes more pressure from the top? It becomes a vicious circle until something gives. Anarchy results. That is why God's system of authority is never based on force but on love and submission—all members being in submission to each other.

Christ loves the church and gave His life for it. Husbands are to love their wives as Christ loved the church and as they love their own bodies. Have you ever seen a man cutting up his own body for pleasure? Not if he is sane. Have you ever seen a man disregard even the least little scratch on his body? This is the care a man should have for his own body and his wife and the care a pastor should have for his congregation.

Jesus has this kind of care for the universal church and the local pastor stands in the same position over the church body under his care. He should exercise his authority in the love of God.

Pastors, never take the attitude that you do not need every member of your congregation. Sheep, members of the congregation, never take the attitude that you do not need the pastor, the shepherd, whom God has set in the local church for your good.

Chapter 5

Defining the Offices

Chapter 5

❧

Defining the Offices

We have already seen that the office of the pastor is chosen by God. God the Father and the Lord Jesus Christ choose men as pastors (1 Corinthians 12:28; Ephesians 4:8, 11). Now let us see what pastors do and what each of the offices under the pastor does. Let us first look at the Greek words for each of the offices we are going to study and see what they mean.

The word for pastor is *poimen,* and it means a shepherd; the pastor is the one who appoints elders. And the word for elder is *presbuteros*, meaning someone who is mature. The office of an elder requires more than just being mature in the Word. We will discuss his qualifications later.

The word for bishop is *episkopos*, which is a compound word in the Greek. It comes from *epi-* meaning "over," and *skopos* meaning "to view or to see." It is self-explanatory, meaning an overseer. The last office in the local church is that of the deacon, which comes from the word *diakonos,* meaning to minister. Now let us examine the office or function of each of these ministries.

The Pastor

God did not use the titles *pastor* and *shepherd* without purpose. The first quality of a pastor is that he is the leader. He heads his flock and makes decisions concerning them. His main function is to find pasture for them. He teaches them the Word of God. He may not be smart in every area of church operations, but he is gifted with a teaching ability. He needs to spend much time in the Word and in prayer to feed his gift and mature in his office.

Every pastor should be aware that many in his congregation are more intelligent in some areas than he is. Many of them have great expertise in natural fields and can benefit him through counsel. He must remain teachable. Some of them may even be more mature in the Word than he is. But if he leans on the anointing that accompanies his office, he can always successfully fill his place as pastor and leader of the flock. The abilities of the Holy Spirit accompany every ministry gift (Romans 11:29).

Now let us look at some Scriptures that deal with the office of pastor. Let us begin with 1 Peter 5:1–4:

> *The elders which are among you I exhort, who am also an elder, and a witness of the sufferings*

of Christ, and also a partaker of the glory that shall be revealed: Feed the flock of God which is among you, taking the oversight thereof, not by constraint, but willingly, not for filthy lucre, but of a ready mind; Neither as being lords over God's heritage, but being ensamples to the flock. And when the chief Shepherd shall appear, ye shall receive a crown of glory that fadeth not away.

Did you notice that the word *pastor* is not mentioned here? So you may ask, how do we know we are discussing a pastor? By context. Peter began by exhorting the elders. Notice that it is plural. Peter also pointed out that he is an elder [*presbuteros*]. In verse two, however, he said, *"feed the flock of God."* Immediately, we know he was talking about pastors, because the Greek word here for *"feed"* is *poimen* (pastor or shepherd). So verse two should read, "Shepherd the flock of God which is among you." Who is the shepherd? The pastor. In this passage then, we have Peter calling the pastor an elder. That makes sense. The pastor should be mature in the Word of God, in spiritual matters. You would not want someone without maturity in the pastorate of your church.

What you have to understand in the Word of God is that the term *elder* is quite freely used for the office of pastor. The context indicates that. When the pastor is called an elder, he is clearly different from the other elders. He stands as chief elder.

The next indication that Peter was addressing pastors is found in the phrase, *"taking the oversight."*

The word *"oversight"* is *episkopos; bishopric.* There is only one person who can take the oversight of God's flock. He is the pastor, the one chosen by God.

The significant thing about Peter's instruction, however, is that he told the pastor that he has to take the initiative. We should see that God is putting the responsibility for leadership on the pastor's shoulders. The pastor does not say, "Lord, let the congregation know this or that." God speaks to the pastor and tells him what the congregation should hear. But notice that the instruction is a command. *"Take the oversight."* He is telling the pastor to have some gumption, to take leadership of the church.

But there are some qualifications given to this charge. First, the pastor is to take the office *"willingly"* rather than *"by constraint." Constraint* here means "of necessity." A pastor should never take his position because he feels he has to. When God calls a pastor, he gives him a pastor's heart, the desire to help people spiritually. So the next qualification has to do with the man's motives. He is not to take the pastor's office for *"filthy lucre."* This means money is not to be his reason for accepting the job. Some people might think a pastor should not make much money. I will show you later from the Word of God that he ought to be paid well for dedicating himself to his calling.

The next instruction is very important. The pastor is not to be a dictator: *"Neither as being lords over God's heritage."* Look at that carefully. Whose heritage? God's. How is one to be over the flock? As an example. That is what *"ensamples"* means. A pastor leads, and he does not tell his congregation to do anything he would not do himself, both in word and deed.

One of the beautiful things this passage shows is the chain of command in the local church. Notice that verse four says that when the Chief Shepherd, who is Jesus, appears, He will reward the pastor. The word for shepherd is *poimen*. So Jesus identifies himself with the pastor. But in the same way, notice that the pastor is called an elder and, by implication in verse two, a bishop, also. If Jesus is called the Chief Shepherd, then the pastor ought to be called the chief elder and the chief bishop in the local church. Jesus is a pastor, but not all pastors are Jesus. The pastor is an elder, but not all elders (or bishops) are the pastor. A pastor must maintain the qualities of those below him.

Let us look at the pastor's heart again. *"Neither as being lords over God's heritage."* Whose heritage? God's. Go back to verse two: *"feed the flock of God."* It should be clear that the pastor does not own the flock in any sense; he merely has responsibility over it. Moses watched Jethro's sheep. He was the shepherd, but the sheep belonged to Jethro. For the pastor who understands that, it is a great freedom. The sheep belong to God. The pastor always has recourse in the owner. He can always talk to the owner about the sheep and their problems. The owner will take care of the things the shepherd cannot handle.

In the local congregation, it is also clear that the people do not ultimately answer to the pastor; they answer to God. He owns the sheep. The pastor's responsibility is to admonish them and feed them from the Word of God. Once the people walk out the door, whether or not they live the Word is their responsibility. That does not mean the pastor has no concern for them; he simply cannot dictate to them. He can encourage and exhort them, but he cannot watch over their lives. Have you ever seen people suddenly stop talking when a pastor walks into the room? If you talk about things you would not want the pastor to hear, then you ought to remember that the "chief pastor," the Lord Jesus Christ, hears every word you say. He never leaves you nor forsakes you.

To further validate what we saw in 1 Peter, let us look to Paul for another Scripture where the pastor is called an elder. In Acts 20:17–28, Paul met with the elders of Ephesus. In verse seventeen we read this:

And from Miletus he sent to Ephesus, and called the elders of the church.

The reason that *"elders"* is plural and *"Ephesus"* is singular is that there were many churches in Ephesus. The churches were not like they are today. They were not large congregations. Most of them met in homes. We know these elders were pastors from what Paul said to them in verse twenty-eight:

Take heed therefore unto yourselves, and to all the flock, over which the Holy Ghost hath made you

overseers, to feed the church of God, which he hath
purchased with his own blood.

Now, several things ought to be leaping out at you for their similarity to what Peter said. First, who made these elders to be overseers? The Holy Spirit did. Therefore, Paul had to be addressing pastors because the office of a bishop is something a man aspires to (1 Timothy 3:1). It is not a ministry gift given by the Lord Jesus Christ (Ephesians 4:11). We see here that the pastor is called the overseer in his congregation. Accordingly, he has authority over all the elders and bishops under him and is the one who chooses them. The final evidence in this verse is that Paul said to feed the flock of God. The word *"feed"* is the word *poimen*, which means to pastor. Again, the flock belongs to God. The purchase price is the blood of the Lord Jesus Christ. Whoever purchases, owns.

Now let us go on to the next office under the pastor: the elder.

The Elder

The first point to establish is that there is a multiplicity of elders in the local church. In James 5:14, we saw that the elders (plural) in the church (singular) are to be called to minister to the sick. Recall in Acts 14:23 that Paul and Barnabas had also *"ordained them elders in every church."* Titus was also told to *"ordain elders in every city"* (Titus 1:5). An interesting point arises here. As far as I can see in God's Word, pastors were not ordained. I am not saying they should not be. It simply appears that they were ordained when they were in the office of elder. When they had proven themselves in that ministry, then God promoted them to a higher office.

Perhaps the most well-known Scriptures that show the relationship of elders to ministry offices are found in chapter fifteen of Acts. Notice verses one and two:

> *And certain men which came down from Judaea taught the brethren, and said, Except ye be circumcised after the manner of Moses, ye cannot be saved. When therefore Paul and Barnabas had no small dissension and disputation with them, they determined that Paul and Barnabas, and certain other of them, should go up to Jerusalem unto the apostles and elders about this question.*

Here we see again that there were elders (plural) at Jerusalem. They were a group distinct from the apostles. Again, the ministers and elders are seen working together in verses twenty-two and twenty-three:

> *Then pleased it the apostles and elders, with the whole church, to send chosen men of their own company to Antioch with Paul and Barnabas; namely, Judas surnamed Barsabas, and Silas, chief men among the brethren: and they wrote letters by them after this manner; The apostles and elders and brethren send greeting unto the*

*brethren which are of the Gentiles in Antioch and
Syria and Cilicia.*

These apostles were in Jerusalem and worked
together with the elders. During the dispute about
whether to keep the law or not, Peter became the
spokesman for the apostles (verse seven). Then in
verse thirteen, James arose as the spokesman for the
elders. Apparently, James was the chief elder, the
pastor. The pastor of any congregation is the chief
elder. From other historical facts surrounding the
book of Acts, it was reported that James was the
pastor at Jerusalem. Acts 21:18 also seems to prove
this.

*And the day following Paul went in with us unto
James; and all the elders were present.*

It is very interesting that for this important meeting James had all his elders present. All the rest of
the men were called *"elders,"* but James was distin-
guished from among them all by reason of his office.
James was the chief elder or pastor. He ruled over
many other elders in the church. The elders are to
assist the pastor with the spiritual oversight of the
church.

Let us look more closely at the function or responsibility of elders in the church.

*Remember them which have the rule over you,
who have spoken unto you the word of God:
whose faith follow, considering the end of their
conversation.*   (Hebrews 13:7)

In this verse, the key words are *"rule,"* *"spoken,"* and *"Word of God."* These words indicate the function of the elder's office in the local church. Anyone who is mature in the Lord is an elder. But the office of an elder is different. The main function of the elder's office is that he rules and teaches. He shares the pastor's responsibility. He rules and teaches in the local church. These are his functions.

Compare 1 Thessalonians 5:12 for these same responsibilities:

> *And we beseech you, brethren, to know them which labor among you, and are over you in the Lord, and admonish you.*

In this verse, the words *"over you"* represent the ruling, and the words *"admonish you"* signify the teaching responsibility.

Another Scripture that shows these responsibilities is 1 Timothy 3:1–5. Do not let the word *"bishop"* in verse one confuse you. A bishop is, first of all, an elder who gains responsibility. He must stand in the office of an elder to become a bishop. Notice his responsibilities:

> *This is a true saying, If a man desire the office of a bishop, he desireth a good work. A bishop then must be...apt to teach....One that ruleth well his own house, having his children in subjection with all gravity, (For if a man know not how to rule his own house, how shall he take care of the church of God?).* (vv. 1–2, 4–5)

So, the word *"bishop"* here refers to an elder who rules and teaches in the local church.

First Timothy 5:17 is another Scripture that clarifies these two functions:

> *Let the elders that rule well be counted worthy of double honor, especially they who labor in the word and doctrine*

Here, we are again talking about ruling and teaching, and this verse is specifically talking about the pastor as the chief elder. But the qualifications for a pastor also fit the qualifications for an elder. Do you remember when we spoke of a pastor being well paid? That is what *"double honor"* refers to. Some people would have you think that it means double reward in heaven some day, or double respect. But it means double salary for those who labor in the Word and doctrine. Study is work.

How do I derive that? Well, look at verse eighteen:

> *For the Scripture saith, Thou shalt not muzzle the ox that treadeth out the corn. And, The laborer is worthy of his reward.*

The word *"labor"* in verse seventeen speaks not only of diligent effort, but also of an occupation. The pastor is the only one in the church whose full occupation is the labor of the Word. Being worthy of one's reward (v. 18) refers to salary. The analogy of the ox relates to the pastor's work. He treads out the grain for the benefit of the people. The corn represents what they bring into the storehouse: their tithes and offerings. As he labors in the storehouse ruling and teaching, he has a right to draw his salary from the giving of the people. So, to be worthy of double honor means that a pastor who feeds his people and tends them well should be paid well. He should receive double honor over other elders, associates, and leaders in the church.

A pastor who works just for the money is not going to fulfill what God has called him to do. The double honor should not influence his decision to pastor or not (1 Peter 5:2).

Another Scripture that I want to consider in light of the elder's function is Titus 2:1–3.

> But speak thou the things which become sound doctrine: That the aged men be sober, grave, temperate, sound in faith, in charity, in patience. The aged women likewise, that they be in behavior as becometh holiness, not false accusers, not given to much wine, teachers of good things.

As we have already seen in verse one, *"speak thou the things which become sound doctrine"* has reference to teaching. But something else comes up in these verses that we have not seen before. The word for *"aged men,"* in the Greek, is *presbuteros,* or elder. But surprisingly, in verse three, *"aged women"* is the same word, only it is in the feminine gender. So it is apparent that a church is not out of scriptural order to have elderesses who rule and teach in the church. A church would be scriptural with all men elders, but it would be just as scriptural to have men and women serving as elders. In fact, if you come to visit the church that I pastor on a communion Sunday, do not be surprised to be served by a woman. Women serve communion, teach children's and women's classes, and minister from the pulpit.

Immediately, I can hear some of you saying, "But Paul said a woman is not allowed to teach in the church." Let us look at that in 1 Timothy 2:12:

> *But I suffer not a woman to teach, nor to usurp authority over the man, but to be in silence.*

The word *"over"* is the key word here. The woman is not allowed to overrule the man in teaching. Neither is she to usurp his authority. There are several possible meanings here, but I personally read this verse this way: I see *"the man"* as a reference to the pastor. The pastor can allow a woman to teach. She cannot usurp his authority. Nowhere in the Word do I find a precedent for a woman to be a pastor. While many of us know women who have been pastors, and successful ones, I personally do not think they have stood in the office of the pastor. I think God used them in the office of elderesses because He could not get a man to respond to the call. Every other ministry gift in the Word of God can be filled by women. There are scriptural examples of women apostles, prophetesses, evangelists, and teachers. God compares the pastor/congregation relationship to a marriage. The pastor is the head. He is not setting precedent for a woman to be the head of a marriage or a church. Enough said.

Let us go on to the office of deacon and then come back briefly to illustrate the office of bishop.

The Deacon

The office of deacon was established in Acts chapter six. I am not going to deal with the office of deacon at length here. Let us look at Acts 6:1–4 to establish the qualifications and function of deacons:

> *And in those days, when the number of the disciples was multiplied, there arose a murmuring of the Grecians against the Hebrews, because their widows were neglected in the daily ministration* [diakonos]. *Then the twelve called the multitude of the disciples unto them, and said, It is not reason that we should leave the word of God, and serve* [diakonos] *tables. Wherefore, brethren, look ye out among you seven men of honest report, full of the Holy Ghost and wisdom, whom we may appoint over this business. But we will give ourselves continually to prayer, and to the ministry* [diakonos] *of the word.*

In verse one, we see that as soon as the church was formed, problems arose because there was spiritual immaturity in the church. Here, the Holy Spirit set the priorities for problem solving in the local congregation. Notice in verse one that the word *"ministration"* comes from the Greek word *diakonos* or deaconing. The word *deacon* means to minister or serve. We will come to a study of the deacon's qualifications. You should notice that there are spiritual qualifications for those who serve in the church. It is not just a matter of waiting tables or serving in other capacities. To serve in the church is a spiritual service as is pointed out by this passage.

Look at the way the word *deacon* is used in the passage. The apostles said it did not make sense for them to leave the Word of God to deacon tables. On the contrary, they would give themselves continually to prayer and to the deaconing of the Word.

I want you to see something here. Anything that is of service to the people is deaconing. The pastor is the servant of the Lord Jesus Christ, but he ministers or deacons to the people. What does he minister or deacon? The Word of God. The obligation of the pastor is to continually give himself to prayer and the deaconing of the Word. What I want you to see about the pastor is that he is a combination of all the offices under him. The pastor has been called an elder, a bishop, and is now seen as a deacon. Within the pastor's office itself is a clear outline of the chain of command for the local congregation.

You also should realize that Jesus Christ is at the top of the ladder of authority. Below him is the pastor. Below the pastor are the bishops and elders. Below them are the deacons. It is interesting that from the top down, each office is a combination of all the offices below. The Lord Jesus Christ is the summation of all the offices below Him. The pastor's office contains all the functions of the offices below him, and so on. This is a pattern of delegated authority. To be a good leader, you must know how to be a good follower.

Let us go on to the office of bishop now.

The Bishop

In Titus 1:5–6, we saw that Paul instructed Titus to ordain elders in every city. In verses seven through nine though, he began to give the qualifications for a bishop or overseer. Why is that? A bishop oversees other elders. He is an elder with added responsibility. You will see in 1 Timothy 3:1–7 that the bishop's qualifications are the same as the elder in Titus 1:5–9. Both are required to have the same qualities of maturity and knowledge of God's Word. They both rule and teach.

Let me give you an example from my church. My assistant pastor is a bishop. When he came to my church years ago, he was recognized for his maturity in the Word of God. The pastor then began to have him counsel. Then he was given more responsibility and ruled over others assigned to him. He also took on classes and began to teach. So, he officially stood in the office of a bishop. A bishop has more responsibility in the church than an elder. The same is true for what is traditionally called a Sunday school superintendent. Ours began teaching. He showed himself faithful in that office and was moved up. With each promotion he proved himself trustworthy and faithful until at last he stood in the office of bishop. He now oversees all the other elders who teach in the church. Notice that the qualifications for the bishop include proven reliability and character. Titus 1:7 begins, *"For a bishop must be blameless, as the steward of God,"* and 1 Timothy 3:2 starts the same way: *"A bishop then must be blameless."*

We have defined the offices within the local church. Now let us look more closely at the qualifications for the offices.

Chapter 6

The Qualifications for Office

Chapter 6

❦

The Qualifications for Office

Whenever a congregation grows, the same needs arise for the pastor as arose for the apostles in Jerusalem. They are called to be continually before the Lord. Therefore, certain responsibilities have to be taken up by mature believers in the congregation. The pastor is to deacon, or minister the Word of God to the believers. I am sure all pastors feel the same as I do; they want to present the very best to their people. To do this, they have to be free from the responsibilities that deacons and elders should carry. Church offices should give full allegiance to the pastor as long as he maintains his integrity and does not blatantly violate scriptural principles. How elders and deacons follow the vision and direction of the pastor is how they ultimately follow the Lord. Let us see what the Word of God says on qualifications for the men chosen to serve the people and assist the pastor.

Elders and Bishops

I am going to talk about these offices together because a bishop must first be an elder. After proving himself in that office he can be given more responsibility as a bishop. We have seen that the word *presbuteros* (elder) indicates someone who is mature in God's Word. The qualifications for these offices are found in 1 Timothy 3:1–7 and Titus 1:7–9. I am going to present a list of those qualifications as taken from the New International Version of the Bible, because it makes some things clearer. Then we will come back and comment on certain points. All men and women chosen for the office of elder should be:

(1) above reproach

(2) the husband (wife) of but one wife (husband)

(3) temperate

(4) self-controlled

(5) respectable

(6) given to hospitality

(7) able to teach

(8) not given to much wine

(9) not violent

(10) not a lover of money

(11) patient

(12) not quarrelsome

(13) not covetous

(14) able to manage his or her own family well

(15) not a recent convert

(16) having a good reputation in the community

(17) a good steward

(18) not self-willed, but submissive

(19) a lover of what is good

(20) upright

(21) holy

(22) disciplined

These are the qualifications of godliness and ability required of elders in the church.

There is one of these qualifications that needs to be amplified because there has been confusion and debate about it in many church circles. Number two says a man must be the husband of but one wife, or one wife at a time. It does not say he is never to have been married before. It is perfectly clear in God's Word that divorce is sanctioned in certain cases (Deuteronomy 24:1; Matthew 5:32).

If a person does divorce for these reasons, he or she is free to remarry without sin (Deuteronomy 24:2; 1 Corinthians 7:15, 28). The restriction on this office refers to polygamy, which was practiced in many societies at the time.

Timothy is an example of the ordination of elders. Timothy was ordained through the laying on of hands. God put the ministry gift in him (Ephesians 4:11; 1 Corinthians 12:28), and the elders laid hands on him as a witness. They recognized his calling. Ministry gifts are not given by the laying on of hands. The anointing that comes with the laying on of hands may help to stir up the gift from God that is in you, but it does not put it there. Neither can prophecy put the gift in you. Prophecy merely confirms what God has already done in your spirit.

Let us examine 1 Timothy 1:18 and 4:14 in this light:

> *This charge I commit unto thee, son Timothy, according to the prophecies which went before on thee, that thou by them mightest war a good warfare;...Neglect not the gift that is in thee, which was given thee by prophecy, with the laying on of the hands of the presbytery.*

The ministry gift that Paul pointed out here was one that was given by God the Father and the Lord Jesus Christ. Again I emphasize, we do not lay hands on someone and make him an apostle. We do not lay hands on someone and make him a pastor. The laying on of hands becomes a point of contact and of dedication. The Holy Spirit ministers anointing through the laying on of hands. The anointing will energize the ministry gift that is already there. Laying on of hands always represents the ministry of the supernatural, not of the calling itself.

Let us look at 2 Timothy 1:6:

> *Wherefore I put thee in remembrance that thou stir up the gift of God, which is in thee by the putting on of my hands.*

I like what the New International Version says here. It says, *"I remind you to fan into flame the gift of God, which is in you through the laying on of my hands."* Elders and pastors should do what the Holy Spirit instructed Timothy to do. They should stir up that gift. It is up to you to do the stirring and the fanning of that gift.

You have to remember that the Word of God says that many are called but few are chosen (Matthew 22:14). Why is that? Many people have the calling down inside them, but few of them do anything with it. It is up to you to continue studying God's Word and praying so that God can use that ministry gift. Just keep feeding on the Word and praying in the Spirit, and God can open a door. God will be able to use you.

Now let us see what qualifies a deacon for service to the congregation.

The Deacon

Let us go back to Acts chapter six to see what qualifications God requires in those who serve as deacons.

Wherefore, brethren, look ye out among you seven men of honest report, full of the Holy Ghost and wisdom, whom we may appoint over this business.....And the saying pleased the whole multitude: and they chose Stephen, a man full of faith and of the Holy Ghost, and Philip, and Prochorus, and Nicanor, and Timon, and Parmenas, and Nicolas a proselyte of Antioch: Whom they set before the apostles: and when they had prayed, they laid their hands on them.

(Acts 6:3, 5–6)

Notice what was said of Stephen. He was full of the Holy Spirit, and he was full of faith. Where does faith come from? From hearing the Word of God. Therefore, Stephen was full of the Word. Jude twenty tells us that we build ourselves up on our faith by praying in tongues. Apparently, Stephen prayed in the spirit. He was full of the Holy Spirit. Deacons need to be filled with the Spirit and the Word. This brings faith and power. That is what to look for in a church when you appoint men and women into service.

But there is another place where qualifications are listed for the office of deacon. I have again taken this list from the New International Version. It is found in 1 Timothy 3:8–12. There it says the deacon must be:

(1) worthy of respect

(2) sincere

(3) not indulging in much wine

(4) not pursuing dishonest gain

(5) keeping hold of the deep truths of the faith with a clear conscience

(6) first tested

(7) married to one worthy of respect—the wife of a deacon is not to be a malicious talker, is to be temperate and trustworthy in everything, and is to be able to manage her children and household well

(8) the husband of but one wife

If a deacon meets these qualifications then he can serve as a deacon. The sixth qualification is an interesting one, and I believe that the testing of a deacon is that he should meet the standards of Acts chapter six. He is to be full of the Holy Spirit and full of faith, able to use his knowledge of the Word of God, which is being full of wisdom.

There is one other thing I want you to see. Deacons can be either men or women. Look at Romans 16:1–2:

> *I commend unto you Phebe our sister, which is a servant* [diakonos] *of the church which is at Cenchrea: That ye receive her in the Lord, as becometh saints, and that ye assist her in whatsoever business she hath need of you: for she hath been a succourer of many, and of myself also.*

Phoebe was a servant in the church of Cenchrea. She was a deacon. The Greek word is *diakonos,* deacon, only here it is in the feminine gender, a deaconess. What did she do? She was a *"succourer of many."* That simply means she was a helper of many. So deacons and deaconesses help the many or the congregation. As I said before, if you visit a church that I pastor, do not be surprised if you find the traditional work of a deacon being done by men and women.

Now it would seem that we have covered all the qualifications for the offices of elder, bishop, and deacon and have said nothing about the qualifications of a pastor. But you will recall that in 1 Peter chapter five and in Acts chapter twenty we saw that the pastor was also called an elder and a bishop. Then we saw that in Acts chapter six they deacon the Word of God to the people. So we can easily see that the pastor must meet all the qualifications of every office below him. But in addition to having proven himself in this way, he also has a divine call on his life from God the Father and the Lord Jesus Christ. This call is supernatural. A man can aspire to be an elder or bishop, a sheep over sheep. But it takes a miracle to turn a sheep into a shepherd. Elders can assist. But they are not the pastor.

In the case of the service of the body of Christ in each of these offices, dedication and faithfulness are the qualities that will make a person a success. So if you desire to serve God in your local church, study what God requires. Then serve Him and the people with a willing heart.

Chapter 7

The Aim of the Pastor's Office

Chapter 7

The Aim of the Pastor's Office

Since the pastor is the head of the local church, his office is obviously the most important, and his function must be a success if the church is to have the supernatural movement of God. That is the aim of his calling. But how do you get God to move in a body of believers? I think the answer to that is back in Ephesians 4:11–12:

And he gave some, apostles, and some, prophets; and some, evangelists; and some, pastors and teachers; For the perfecting of the saints, for the work of the ministry, for the edifying of the body of Christ.

Now if you read this as it appears here in the King James Version, you can get the idea that the pastor is to do everything in the local church. He is to perfect the saints, he is to do the work of ministry, and he is to edify the body of Christ. From what we saw of James 5:14, however, there seems to be a contradiction, because the mature believers who stand in the office of elder are out doing the work of the ministry by laying hands on the sick. Maybe this verse should read differently.

Let us remove the first comma in verse twelve and see what that does. Now we find that the pastor is to perfect the saints so that they can do the work of the ministry. This makes more sense when we find that verse thirteen gives us the goal of Christian growth: to come to the fullness of Christ's own stature.

That is different than playing church is it not? You see, it is up to the pastor to equip the saints with the knowledge of God's Word that will enable them to go out and do the work of the ministry.

I want to look at two passages in the Word of God that show how Paul fulfilled this responsibility.

When Paul addressed the pastors of Ephesus at Miletus, he told them he had fulfilled his responsibility to them. What Paul said to them is a guideline for pastors in the work of perfecting the saints. Let us look at Acts chapter twenty again.

> *And when they were come to him, he said unto them, Ye know, from the first day that I came into Asia, after what manner I have been with you at all seasons, Serving the Lord with all humility of mind, and with many tears, and temptations, which befell me by the lying in wait of the Jews: And how I kept back nothing that was profitable unto you, but have showed you, and have taught*

you publicly, and from house to house,...Wherefore I take you to record this day, that I am pure from the blood of all men. For I have not shunned to declare unto you all the counsel of God. Take heed therefore unto yourselves, and to all the flock, over the which the Holy Ghost hath made you overseers, to feed the church of God, which he hath purchased with his own blood.

(Acs 20:18–20, 26–28)

In his words to the assembly of pastors before him, Paul first encouraged them by telling them of the trials he had faced and had overcome. Then he told them that they were responsible for their own spiritual progress. Why? Because he had kept back nothing that was profitable for them. The Greek word for *"kept back"* is used two different ways in the Greek. One way means to keep food from a starving man, and the other means to furl the sails on a ship. What happens when you furl the sails on a ship? It slows down. So what Paul is saying is that each time he came to them, he gave them the whole counsel of God. That was like letting down spiritual sails so that the people could catch every breath of the Holy Spirit. That is what the Word does. It opens you up to the inspiration of the Holy Spirit.

Now there is one thing you should remember. You have the same Holy Spirit in you as Oral Roberts, Kenneth Hagin, and Billy Graham. These men in the ministry offices have supernatural gifts by which they receive revelation knowledge of God's Word for the purpose of passing it on to believers.

The responsibility of the pastor begins when he receives revelation from the Holy Spirit, and it does not end until he passes it on to his congregation. If he fails to do that, he then becomes responsible for their failures. Their blood is on his hands.

Paul said he had proclaimed the whole counsel of God in public and also in the homes of the believers. He had held nothing back. Their blood could not be on his hands. So Paul told the pastors the same thing. They are not to keep anything back from their congregations.

Another passage that shows how this works is in 2 Corinthians 6:11–13. Let us see what that says in this context:

> O ye Corinthians, our mouth is open unto you, our heart is enlarged. Ye are not straitened in us, but ye are straitened in your own bowels. Now for a recompence in the same, (I speak as unto my children,) be ye also enlarged.

What was Paul trying to say? First of all, notice that the mouth is opened only after the heart is enlarged. Well, what does it mean to have your heart enlarged? It is the same thing that was taught back in Joshua 1:8. God said to meditate in the Word day and night. The Word of God should be continuously in your mouth. By meditating in the Word, your heart becomes enlarged with the Word. Then when you open your mouth to teach, you will be giving out the Word of God. Out of the abundance (largeness) of the heart, the mouth speaks.

Then he says that they were not *"straitened"* in him. The word *"straitened"* means "hindered by." So we can read verse twelve like this: "You are hindered by your own bowels." Well, what are bowels? Throughout the Word of God, the word *bowels* refers to the emotions. Do you remember in Genesis when Joseph was delivered out of prison and became the Prime Minister of Egypt? If you recall, all his brothers came down to buy food in Egypt from Joseph. They did not recognize him. He went into a back room to cry so he would not give himself away. It says his bowels yearned over his brothers (Genesis 43:30). It was a tremendously emotional time for Joseph.

Now let us get back to 2 Corinthians 6:12. What Paul was saying is that these believers were hindered by their own emotions. Start in verse eleven again. Paul said that these people were not hindered spiritually by him because he had taught them everything that was in his heart. He had not spared anything. If Paul had taught them everything he knew, then what was holding them back; what kept them from unfurling their own sails and taking off? He said they were hindered by their own emotions. Today we would say they were letting their emotions push them around. When your heart is not full of the Word of God, you are subject to your own feelings and emotions and they will rule you. The worst kind of Christian is one who is living by feelings. They get inspired in church, but the feelings do not last. After hearing a very inspirational message, the feelings wear off and there is nothing left.

Have you ever wondered why the Greek lists pastors and teachers together as a single ministry gift in Ephesians 4:11? A pastor-teacher? When a pastor-teacher feeds his people the Word, when the inspiration of the service goes away and the emotions settle, the Word stays in your heart. Your heart remains enlarged, and you are not hindered by your emotions. You begin to live by the Word of God and not by how you feel. Paul was not controlled by his emotions.

Am I saying that it is wrong to have emotions? No. I am saying that it is wrong to live by emotions. I love to get excited about the Word of God. In fact, sometimes I get so excited I cannot contain it and just run out of my office and up and down the sanctuary. Hey, that is a great emotional feeling. But when that is gone, the Word is still in my heart.

Do you see why Paul could tell the pastors from Ephesus that he was not responsible for them any longer? He had taught them all he knew to teach them, so they had to take up from there. *"Take heed to yourselves"* meant they had to apply the counsel of God to themselves and to pass it on to their congregations so the people could walk by the spirit and the Word and not by their feelings.

About the Author

About the Author

B ob Yandian is a pastor, international teacher, and founder of the School of the Local Church (a one-year ministerial training school). Bob began pastoring Grace Fellowship in 1980. The church is located in Tulsa, Oklahoma and has grown tremendously to over 3,000 members.

Bob is a graduate of Trinity Bible College where he studied under Charles Duncomb, an associate of Smith Wigglesworth. He also studied Greek at Southwestern College in Oklahoma City. In addition, Bob's background includes several years with Kenneth Hagin Ministries and Rhema Bible Training Center, where he was an instructor and held the position of Dean of Instructors.

Bob is a pastor's pastor who is renowned for his detailed expository teaching of the Word of God as well as his diverse topical instruction. His extensive study of the Scriptures enables him to communicate the uncomprimised Word of God with a strong anointing and practical wisdom.

Through his years of ministry, Bob has taught throughout the United States and Canada as well as Europe, Latin America, Africa, and Asia. He has authored over twenty books covering various topics and teachings. He has also fostered many ministries through The School of the Local Church, which he founded in 1985.

Bob Yandian Ministries is an outreach to people all around the world through radio, television, and the Internet. Bob's vision is to train up the saints to do the work of the ministry. The distribution of his anointed teaching material enables him to fulfill this vision. This ministry is accomplished through sales of Bob's books and tapes, as well as love gifts from valued friends and partners.

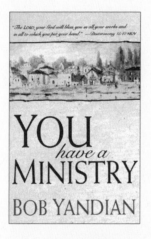